# All the Days of Lent

Scripture, thoughts and
things to do during

# All the Days of Lent

Colane Recker, O.S.F.

Art by Joyce Stanley

Ave Maria Press ~ Notre Dame, Indiana 46556

Acknowledgments:

*The New American Bible,* © 1970 by the Confraternity of Christian Doctrine, Washington, D.C. For short scriptural quotations introducing meditations. Used by permission of copyright owner. All rights reserved.

Darton, Longman & Todd, Ltd., and Doubleday & Company, Inc. *The Jerusalem Bible.* © 1966. For scriptural readings at the end of meditations.

International Committee on English in the Liturgy, Inc. For excerpts from the English translation of *The Roman Missal.* © 1973.

The Liturgical Press. For four prayers from the *Book of Prayer,* 4th ed. revised. © 1975.

Library of Congress Catalog Card Number: 78-73825

International Standard Book Number: 0-87793-168-2

Art and design: Joyce Stanley

Printed and bound in the United States of America.

**Remember, man, you are dust, and to dust you will return.**

**THOUGHT:**

Ashes have always reminded God's people that they will not live forever. God does control our lives and he alone knows when we will be freed to join him.

**TODAY:**

Make two positive Lenten resolutions that you have a chance of keeping.

## READ AND MEDITATE ON JOHN 17:1-5.

After saying this, Jesus raised his eyes to heaven and said:
"Father, the hour has come:
glorify your Son
so that your Son may glorify you;
and, through the power over all mankind that you have given
    him,
let him give eternal life to all those you have entrusted to him.
And eternal life is this:
to know you,
the only true God,
and Jesus Christ whom you have sent.
I have glorified you on earth
and finished the work
that you gave me to do.
Now, Father, it is time for you to glorify me
with the glory I had with you
before ever the world was."

"No follower of mine shall ever walk in darkness; no, he shall possess the light of life," says the Lord (Jn 8:12).

**THOUGHT:**
Have I given myself to be a totally committed Christ-follower?

**TODAY:**
Spend an extra five minutes in prayer, asking for the insight needed to prepare for Easter.

## READ AND MEDITATE ON JOHN 17:6-11.

I have made your name known
to the men you took from the world to give me.
They were yours and you gave them to me,
and they have kept your word.
Now at last they know
That all you have given me comes indeed from you;
for I have given them
the teaching you gave to me,
and they have truly accepted this, that I came from you,
and have believed that it was you who sent me.

I pray for them;
I am not praying for the world
but for those you have given me,
because they belong to you:
all I have is yours
and all you have is mine,
and in them I am glorified.
I am not in the world any longer,
but they are in the world,
and I am coming to you.

Holy Father,
keep those you have given me true to your name,
so that they may be one like us.

Dispensations can be given from fasting; but from love, never.

**THOUGHT:**

We lack sufficient love of our neighbor, both inwardly and outwardly. Our lives are full of self-seeking.

**TODAY:**

Think of someone you have been unkind to. Make an effort to say or do something kind for that person.

**READ AND MEDITATE ON JOHN 17:12-19.**

While I was with them,
I kept those you have given me true to your name.
I have watched over them and not one is lost
except the one who chose to be lost,
and this was to fulfill the scriptures.

But now I am coming to you
and while still in the world I say these things
to share my joy with them to the full.
I passed your word on to them,
and the world hated them,
because they belong to the world
no more than I belong to the world.

I am not asking you to remove them from the world,
but to protect them from the evil one.
They do not belong to the world
any more than I belong to the world.
Consecrate them in the truth;
your word is truth.

As you sent me into the world,
I have sent them into the world,
and for their sake I consecrate myself
so that they too may be consecrated in truth.

When the designated time had come, God sent forth his Son born of a woman, born under the law, to deliver from the law those who were subjected to it, so that we might receive our status as adopted sons (Gal 4:4-5).

**THOUGHT:**

In the story of salvation we must be either builders or destroyers; either we gather or we scatter. There can be no neutrality.

**TODAY:**

Encourage yourself to willingly deny yourself a critical word.

**READ AND MEDITATE ON JOHN 17:20-26.**

I pray not only for these,
but for those also
who through their words will believe in me.
May they all be one.

Father, may they be one in us,
as you are in me and I am in you,
so that the world may believe it was you who sent me.
I have given them the glory you gave to me,
that they may be one as we are one.
With me in them and you in me,
may they be so completely one
that the world will realize that it was you who sent me
and that I have loved them as much as you loved me.

Father, I want those you have given me
to be with me where I am,
so that they may always see the glory
you have given me
because you loved me
before the foundation of the world.

Father, Righteous One,
the world has not known you,
but I have known you,
and these have known
that you have sent me.
I have made your name known to them
and will continue to make it known,
so that the love with which you loved me may be in them,
and so that I may be in them.

# The First Sunday of Lent

**Almighty God, grant that through the annual observance of the Lenten discipline we may advance in knowledge of the mystery of Christ and thereby be molded to holiness of life. This we ask through Christ our Lord** (Book of Prayer).

**THOUGHT:**

The more we die to ourselves during Lent, the closer our lives will come to be more like the life Jesus lived.

**TODAY:**

Just as Jesus spent time in solitude, spend 10 minutes alone with him.

**Treat others the way you would have them treat you** (Mt 7:12).

THOUGHT:

I cannot live my best unless I am in harmony with this thought. It reaches into every activity of every day.

TODAY:

Go to visit someone you've wanted to visit for some time.

READ AND MEDITATE ON JOHN 18:1-7.

After he had said all this, Jesus left with his disciples and crossed the Kedron valley. There was a garden there, and he went into it with his disciples. Judas the traitor knew the place well, since Jesus often met his disciples there, and he brought the cohort to this place together with a detachment of guards sent by the chief priests and the Pharisees, all with lanterns and torches and weapons. Knowing everything that was going to happen to him, Jesus then came forward and said, "Who are you looking for?" They answered, "Jesus the Nazarene." He said, "I am he." Now Judas the traitor was standing among them. When Jesus said, "I am he," they moved back and fell to the ground. He asked them a second time, "Who are you looking for?" They said, "Jesus the Nazarene."

**My house shall be called a house of prayer, but you are turning it into a den of thieves** (Mt 21:13).

**THOUGHT:**

Each of us is a "temple." How do I respect myself? Do I show concern, compassion and love for others in my immediate surroundings?

**TODAY:**

Tell someone you love him (or her), using the three little words "I love you!"

**READ AND MEDITATE ON JOHN 18:8-11.**

"I have told you that I am he," replied Jesus. "If I am the one you are looking for, let these others go." This was to fulfill the words he had spoken, "Not one of those you gave me have I lost."

Simon Peter, who carried a sword, drew it and wounded the high priest's servant, cutting off his right ear. The servant's name was Malchus. Jesus said to Peter, "Put your sword back in its scabbard; am I not to drink the cup that the Father has given me?"

Lord,
look upon us and hear our prayer.
By the good works you inspire,
help us to discipline our bodies
and to be renewed in spirit.
(Opening Prayer)

## THOUGHT:

Changes are a very real part of my life. We can still control these changes and not let them control us.

## TODAY:

Offer a prayer of acceptance for something you can't change right now.

## READ AND MEDITATE ON JOHN 18:12-14.

The cohort and its captain and the Jewish guards seized Jesus and bound him. They took him first to Annas, because Annas was the father-in-law of Caiaphas, who was high priest that year. It was Caiaphas who had suggested to the Jews, "It is better for one man to die for the people."

**Father,**
**without you we can do nothing.**
**By your spirit help us to know what is right**
**and to be eager in doing your work.**
(Opening Prayer)

**THOUGHT:**

I derive happiness by living the life God leads me in. I need to let him enter my life.

**TODAY:**

Decide to forgive yourself of your sins and then resolve to go to confession.

**READ AND MEDITATE ON JOHN 18:15-18.**

Simon Peter, with another disciple, followed Jesus. This disciple, who was known to the high priest, went with Jesus into the high priest's palace, but Peter stayed outside the door. So the other disciple, the one known to the high priest, went out, spoke to the woman who was keeping the door and brought Peter in. The maid on duty at the door said to Peter, "Aren't you another of that man's disciples?" He answered, "I am not." Now it was cold, and the servants and guards had lit a charcoal fire and were standing there warming themselves; so Peter stood there too, warming himself with the others.

**Lord,
may the sacrament you give us
free us from our sinful ways and bring us new life.**
(Prayer after Communion)

**THOUGHT:**

With God, I can leave my sinful ways and find the way to God.
I have faith in his love.

**TODAY:**

What do you worry about most? Make an act of trust in God.

**READ AND MEDITATE ON JOHN 18:19-21.**

The high priest questioned Jesus about his disciples and his
teaching. Jesus answered, "I have spoken openly for all the
world to hear; I have always taught in the synagogue and in
the Temple where all the Jews meet together: I have said
nothing in secret. But why ask me? Ask my hearers what
I taught: they know what I said."

**You are to be a people peculiarly his own, as he promised you** (First Reading).

**THOUGHT:**

Mary was a special person in our salvation history. She is our Mother and a closeness to her is a closeness to Christ.

**TODAY:**

Read the three readings for Sunday's Mass, and prepare to take an active part in the liturgy.

**READ AND MEDITATE ON JOHN 18:22-24.**

At these words, one of the guards standing by gave Jesus a slap in the face, saying, "Is that the way to answer the high priest?" Jesus said, "If there is something wrong in what I said, point it out; but if there is no offense in it, why do you strike me?" Then Annas sent him, still bound, to Caiaphas the high priest.

# The Second Sunday of Lent

**Lord, how good it is for us to be here!** (Gospel)

**THOUGHT:**

God gifted us with our families and friends. I enjoy his gifts and want to spread this joy.

**TODAY:**

Show your joy to another by writing that letter you've been putting off.

Spend 10 minutes alone with Christ again.

**Give and it shall be given to you** (Gospel).

**THOUGHT:**

I give the best that is in me. Generosity should be a natural part of me if I'm really imitating Christ.

**TODAY:**

Instead of tackling anything with an "I have to" spirit, substitute "I want to."

**READ AND MEDITATE ON JOHN 18:25-27.**

As Simon Peter stood there warming himself, someone said to him, "Aren't you another of his disciples?" He denied it saying, "I am not." One of the high priest's servants, a relation of the man whose ear Peter had cut off, said, "Didn't I see you in the garden with him?" Again Peter denied it; and at once a cock crew.

**But do not follow their example. Their words are bold but their deeds are few** (Gospel).

## THOUGHT:

At the heart of each life there is a creative spirit which carries us on to a deeper spirituality, and each experience can be a growing experience.

## TODAY:

When you hear someone criticized, put in a good word for the person.

## READ AND MEDITATE ON JOHN 18:28-32.

They then led Jesus from the house of Caiaphas to the Praetorium. It was now morning. They did not go into the Praetorium themselves or they would be defiled and unable to eat the Passover. So Pilate came outside to them and said, "What charge do you bring against this man?" They replied, "If he were not a criminal, we should not be handing him over to you." Pilate said, "Take him yourselves, and try him by your own law." The Jews answered, "We are not allowed to put a man to death." This was to fulfill the words Jesus had spoken indicating the way he was going to die.

**Father,
teach us to live good lives,
encourage us with your support
and bring us to eternal life.**
(Opening Prayer)

## THOUGHT:

Someone has said that life is like a race. The first laps are easy. Then, it gets a little harder. Finally it becomes a test of endurance to see who stays in and sees it through.

## TODAY:

Make a firm attempt to define your values.

## READ AND MEDITATE ON JOHN 18:33.

So Pilate went back into the Praetorium and called Jesus to him, "Are you the king of the Jews?" he asked.

**More torturous than all else is the human heart, beyond remedy; who can understand it?**
(First Reading)

### THOUGHT:

Each has his own special gift from God. I can learn to "live and let live" if I will remember that no two people are alike.

### TODAY:

Be patient with people who don't agree with you today, and do not press your opinion.

### READ AND MEDITATE ON JOHN 18:34-35.

Jesus replied, "Do you ask this of your own accord, or have others spoken to you about me?" Pilate answered, "Am I a Jew? Is it not your own people and the chief priests who have handed you over to me: what have you done?"

Lord,
may this Communion so change our lives
that we seek more faithfully
the salvation it promises.
(Prayer after Communion)

THOUGHT:

God didn't create us as timid, but as powerful in him. God's power is in me, and through this power I can overcome any and all negations.

TODAY:

Your life is more than it seems to be. Try to direct it positively.

READ AND MEDITATE ON JOHN 18:36.

Jesus replied, "Mine is not a kingdom of this world; if my kingdom were of this world, my men would have fought to prevent my being surrendered to the Jews. But my kingdom is not of this kind."

**I assure you: this day you will be with me in paradise** (Lk 23:43).

**THOUGHT:**

There is no doubt that there is life after death. Heaven consists in God and hell the absence of God.

**TODAY:**

Say a prayer for a happy death for yourself and a loved one.

**READ AND MEDITATE ON JOHN 18:37.**

"So you are a king then?" said Pilate. "It is you who say it," answered Jesus. "Yes, I am a king. I was born for this, I came into the world for this: to bear witness to the truth; and all who are on the side of truth listen to my voice."

# The Third Sunday of Lent

It is precisely in this that God proves his love for us: that while we were still sinners, Christ died for us (Second Reading).

**THOUGHT:**

When we are discouraged by our human weaknesses, we can gain new confidence by remembering God's love.

**TODAY:**

Forget about trying to win the approval of others. Spend 10 minutes alone with Christ.

**God of mercy,
guide us, for we cannot be saved without you.**
(Opening Prayer)

**THOUGHT:**

How often have I prayed for something which God, in his love and mercy, denied me? I must be willing to let God have the final say.

**TODAY:**

Smile when a situation that would normally provoke anger arises today.

**READ AND MEDITATE FOR TEN MINUTES ON JOHN 18:38-40.**

"Truth?" said Pilate "What is that?"; and with that he went out again to the Jews and said, "I find no case against him. But according to a custom of yours I should release one prisoner at the Passover; would you like me, then, to release the king of the Jews?" At this they shouted: "Not this man, but Barabbas." Barabbas was a brigand.

Lord, when my brother wrongs me, how often must I forgive him? Seven times? No, not seven times, but seventy times seven times (Gospel).

## THOUGHT:

After a day or a week, thoughtlessness and unkind words are no longer important. New experiences will enter in if we but let them.

## TODAY:

Forgive a hurt that is a week or more old.

## READ AND MEDITATE ON JOHN 19:1-3.

Pilate then had Jesus taken away and scourged; and after this, the soldiers twisted some thorns into a crown and put it on his head, and dressed him in a purple robe. They kept coming up to him and saying, "Hail, king of the Jews!"; and they slapped him in the face.

**Lord,**
**during this Lenten season**
**nourish us with your word of life**
**and make us one in love and prayer.**
(Opening Prayer)

**THOUGHT:**

**Prayer is one of the most important parts of any spiritual life.**
**Prayer can only become totally God-centered when we put**
**effort into it.**

**TODAY:**

**Evaluate your personal prayer and talk to God about it.**

**READ AND MEDITATE ON JOHN 19:4.**

**Pilate came outside again and said to them, "Look, I am going**
**to bring him out to you to let you see that I find no case."**

**This is what I commanded my people: Listen to my voice; then I will be your God and you shall be my people** (First Reading).

**THOUGHT:**

How marvelous to realize that God has given me eternity. What time binds, eternity sets free. He created me to be his.

**TODAY:**

Try to live this day in the conscious presence of Christ.

READ AND MEDITATE ON LUKE 22:67-69.

They said to him, "If you are the Christ, tell us." "If I tell you," he replied, "you will not believe me, and if I question you, you will not answer. But from now on, the Son of Man will be seated at the right hand of the Power of God."

I will heal their defection,
I will love them freely;
for my wrath is turned away from them.
(First Reading)

**THOUGHT:**

The love of God is a free gift. He will never deprive us of it. When we sin, Christ still loves us. However, he doesn't love the sin.

**TODAY:**

Speak a word of encouragement to someone who seems "down."

**READ AND MEDITATE ON JOHN 19:5.**

Jesus then came out wearing the crown of thorns and the purple robe. Pilate said, "Here is the man."

When the designated time had come, God sent forth his Son born of a woman, born under the law, to deliver from the law those who were subjected to it, so that we might receive our status as adopted sons (Gal 4:4-5).

**THOUGHT:**

Through Mary, we may learn to know and love Jesus more deeply. As a Mother, she cannot be anything but a true guide.

**TODAY:**

Pray the rosary for a greater devotion to Mary.

**READ AND MEDITATE ON JOHN 19:6.**

When they saw him, the chief priests and the guard shouted, "Crucify him! Crucify him!" Pilate said, "Take him yourselves and crucify him: I can find no case against him."

# The Fourth Sunday of Lent

God of kindness and mercy, through your Word you effect in a marvelous way the reconciliation of mankind. Hear our prayer and grant that your Christian people may hasten to the coming feast with ready heart and eager faith (Book of Prayer).

**THOUGHT:**

Lenten time is a perfect season to develop a thankful heart for all Christ suffered for us.

**TODAY:**

Make a list of three things you should be thankful for.
Add to the list each day this week.

The man put his trust in the word Jesus spoke to him, and started for home (Gospel).

THOUGHT:

I have a need to listen to the Word of Christ to me. Christ within is a sure source of direction for my life. I trust in him.

TODAY:

Be a listening post to someone you know who needs to unburden himself.

READ AND MEDITATE ON JOHN 19:7.

"We have a Law," the Jews replied, "and according to that Law he ought to die, because he has claimed to be the Son of God."

**Did the preaching of God's word originate with you? Are you the only ones to whom it has come?**
(I Cor 14:36).

**THOUGHT:**

Is my life lived with too much hurry and confusion? Is it cluttered and full? What part does Jesus have? Only the time when we're too tired even to pray?

**TODAY:**

Help someone without his knowing that it was you.

**READ AND MEDITATE ON JOHN 19:8-9.**

When Pilate heard them say this his fears increased. Reentering the Praetorium, he said to Jesus, "Where do you come from?" But Jesus made no answer.

But, worse still, he was speaking of God as his own Father, thereby making himself God's equal (Gospel).

**THOUGHT:**
Christ never bragged about who he was. He certainly could have. But he subjected his very self to the Father.

**TODAY:**
Be conscious of how you are a blessing from the Father to everyone you meet today.

**READ AND MEDITATE ON JOHN 19:10.**
Pilate then said to him, "Are you refusing to speak to me? Surely you know I have power to release you and I have power to crucify you?"

**Merciful Father,**
**may the penance of our Lenten observance**
**make us your obedient people.**
(Opening Prayer)

**THOUGHT:**

Penance is an essential part of every Lent. A positive penance
is most important. Example: I will do . . . . . . . ., rather than
I will give up . . . . . . . .

**TODAY:**

Review your two Lenten resolutions and renew them if
necessary.

**READ AND MEDITATE ON JOHN 19:11.**

"You would have no power over me," replied Jesus, "if it had
not been given you from above; that is why the one who
handed me over to you has the greater guilt."

**Be kind to one another, compassionate and mutually forgiving, just as God has forgiven you in Christ** (Eph. 4:32).

**THOUGHT:**

People hurt easily. They are sensitive and easily discouraged. I can restore their belief in humanity.

**TODAY:**

Pray that you not be a source of irritation to another.

**READ AND MEDITATE ON JOHN 19:12.**

From that moment Pilate was anxious to set him free, but the Jews shouted, "If you set him free, you are no friend of Caesar's; anyone who makes himself king is defying Caesar."

## Surely the Messiah is not to come from Galilee?
(Gospel)

**THOUGHT:**

Often a person is prejudged because of where he is from or because of his heritage. We should be proud of our parental heritage. But, more important to remember is the fact that we are heirs of God the Father.

**TODAY:**

Thank your families for your heritage, in some way. The best way might be to pass it on.

**READ AND MEDITATE ON JOHN 19:13.**

Hearing these words, Pilate had Jesus brought out, and seated himself on the chair of judgment at a place called the Pavement, in Hebrew Gabbatha.

# The Fifth Sunday of Lent

**Come, let us adore Christ the Lord, who was put to the test and who suffered for us** (Book of Prayer).

**THOUGHT:**

Christ did not back away from suffering. Prayer often won't remove the suffering, but our attitude toward it will. Take your troubles to God.

**TODAY:**

Spend 10 minutes in quiet with the Lord, accepting what you can't change.

**Through her tears she looked up to heaven, for she trusted in the Lord wholeheartedly** (First Reading).

**THOUGHT:**

God has the perfect plan for my life. With God there is no confusion, worry, or tenseness — only peace!

**TODAY:**

Give all your worries and anxieties to the Lord and do not take them back.

**READ AND MEDITATE ON JOHN 19:14.**

It was Passover Preparation Day, about the sixth hour. "Here is your king," said Pilate to the Jews.

**Merciful Lord,**
**we offer this gift of reconciliation**
**so that you will forgive our sins**
**and guide our wayward hearts.**
(Prayer over Gifts)

## THOUGHT:

**Self-condemnation directs my vision downward; if I am to be healed, my vision must be upward toward Christ.**

## TODAY:

**Ask for God's healing power of forgiveness of others and of yourself.**

## READ AND MEDITATE ON JOHN 19:15.

**"Take him away, take him away!" they said. "Crucify him!" "Do you want me to crucify your king?" said Pilate. The chief priests answered, "We have no king except Caesar."**

**Then you will know the truth and the truth will set you free** (Gospel).

**THOUGHT:**

Have I given consent to any limitations? What is keeping me from a deep union with Jesus? No person or thing should have that power.

**TODAY:**

Determine if you are limiting anyone and give him or her freedom to be what he or she ought and not what you want.

**READ AND MEDITATE ON JOHN 19:16-17.**

So in the end Pilate handed him over to them to be crucified. They then took charge of Jesus, and carrying his own cross he went out of the city to the place of the skull or, as it was called in Hebrew, Golgotha.

**Help us to remain faithful to a holy way of life
and guide us to the inheritance you have promised.**
(Opening Prayer)

**THOUGHT:**

In this world, I don't know what tomorrow will bring. But, with God, I know what he has planned for my tomorrow.

**TODAY:**

Treat this day as your very last day on earth — really — and live that way all day.

**READ AND MEDITATE ON JOHN 19:18.**

There they crucified him with two others, one on either side, with Jesus in the middle.

**Lord,**

**grant us your forgiveness
and set us free from our enslavement to sin.**
(Opening Prayer)

### THOUGHT:

Am I a sin addict? Have I allowed sin to become habit in my life? The only way to break such a habit is to put in extra resources.

### TODAY:

Determine what is your particular habit. Go to confession if you haven't been there yet.

### READ AND MEDITATE ON JOHN 19:19-20.

Pilate wrote out a notice and had it fixed to the cross; it ran, "Jesus the Nazarene, King of the Jews." This notice was read by many of the Jews, because the place where Jesus was crucified was not far from the city, and the writing was in Hebrew, Latin and Greek.

**I will be their God, and they shall be my people**
(First Reading).

**THOUGHT:**

To belong to someone means to want what is best for him.
Christ gave us his best — himself.

**TODAY:**

Be calm and quiet for a time, just trying to experience Christ.

**READ AND MEDITATE ON JOHN 19:21-22.**

So the Jewish chief priests said to Pilate, "You should not write
'King of the Jews,' but 'This man said: I am King of the Jews!' "
Pilate answered, "What I have written, I have written."

# Palm Sunday

**Waving our palms, we hurry to pay homage to Jesus as he approaches** (Book of Prayer).

**THOUGHT:**

Christ entered in triumph, but before the week was over, the same city was present at his crucifixion. How fickle the opinion of people.

**TODAY:**

Spend some time in quiet with Jesus, trying to enter into his feelings of the day.

**The poor you always have with you, but me you will not always have** (Gospel).

**THOUGHT:**

Jesus' own people were slow to accept him as God. What prevents him from being complete in my life?

**TODAY:**

Strengthen your determination to keep your resolutions and renew them.

**READ AND MEDITATE ON JOHN 19:23.**

When the soldiers had finished crucifying Jesus they took his clothing and divided it into four shares, one for each soldier. His undergarment was seamless, woven in one piece from neck to hem.

**I tell you solemnly, one of you will betray me** (Gospel).

## THOUGHT:

Judas received 30 pieces of silver for his betrayal. How often I have betrayed Jesus by my sin, for much less.

## TODAY:

Express more thoughtfulness toward someone you work with or live with, someone you find hard to like.

## READ AND MEDITATE ON JOHN 19:24.

The soldiers said to one another, "Instead of tearing it, let's throw dice to decide who is to have it." In this way the words of scripture were fulfilled:
    They shared out my clothing among them.
    They cast lots for my clothes.
This is exactly what the soldiers did.

Father, in your plan of salvation your Son, Jesus, accepted the cross and freed us from the power of the enemy.

THOUGHT:

Do you really appreciate the full meaning of God accepting death for humans? Christ went all the way for me. How dare I hold back?

TODAY:

Be a responsive and appreciative person—don't neglect those who look to you for love and attention.

READ AND MEDITATE ON JOHN 19:25-27.

Near the cross of Jesus stood his mother and his mother's sister, Mary the wife of Clopas, and Mary of Magdala. Seeing his mother and the disciple he loved standing near her, Jesus said to his mother, "Woman, this is your son." Then to the disciple he said, "This is your mother." And from that moment the disciple made a place for her in his home.

Then, taking bread and giving thanks, he broke it, and gave it to them, saying, "This is my Body" (Lk 22:19).

### THOUGHT:

When we love someone, we wish to give something of ourselves. Jesus left us himself — a self that will never change.

### TODAY:

Receive Holy Communion with a special thankfulness.

### READ AND MEDITATE ON LUKE 22:14-20.

When the hour came he took his place at table, and the apostles with him. And he said to them, "I have longed to eat this Passover with you before I suffer; because, I tell you, I shall not eat it again until it is fulfilled in the kingdom of God.

Then, taking a cup, he gave thanks and said, "Take this and share it among you, because from now on, I tell you, I shall not drink wine until the kingdom of God comes."

Then he took some bread, and when he had given thanks, broke it and gave it to them, saying, "This is my body which will be given for you; do this as a memorial of me." He did the same with the cup after supper, and said, "This cup is the new covenant in my blood, which will be poured out for you."

**He humbled himself, obediently accepting even death, death on a cross!** (Phil 2:8).

**THOUGHT:**

Christ had a great peace because he knew he was doing the Father's will. How easy it is to do what I want, but is it what God wants?

**TODAY:**

Forget a personal injury, and remember Christ on the cross for three hours.

Go to the services, if possible.

**Then he rolled a stone across the entrance to the tomb** (Mk 15:46).

**THOUGHT:**

So often obstacles are put in our paths that cause us to be inactive for a time. This period of suffering is necessary for greater growth in Christ, if we accept it as such.

**TODAY:**

Read Mark 15:42-47, slowly and thoughtfully.

It was now evening, and since it was Preparation Day (that is, the vigil of the Sabbath), there came Joseph of Arimathaea, a prominent member of the Council, who himself lived in the hope of seeing the kingdom of God, and he boldly went to Pilate and asked for the body of Jesus. Pilate, astonished that he should have died so soon, summoned the centurion and inquired if he was already dead. Having been assured of this by the centurion, he granted the corpse to Joseph, who bought a shroud, took Jesus down from the cross, wrapped him in the shroud and laid him in a tomb which had been hewn out of the rock. He then rolled a stone against the entrance to the tomb. Mary of Magdala and Mary the mother of Joset were watching and took note of where he was laid.

# Easter
# Sunday

**Why do you search for the Living One among the dead? He is not here; he has been raised up** (Lk 24:6).

**THOUGHT:**

**Christ is risen within me. My spiritual self can be triumphant and glorious. He is my only light.**

**TODAY:**

**Celebrate!**